## All the boring technical jargon:

No portion of this book, either artwork, design, or text or any portion thereof may be reproduced in any form or used in any manner whatsoever without written permission from Kari Denker, except for brief quotations used in reviews. All rights reserved.

Unless otherwise noted, all Scripture quotations are from The Holy Bible, New American Standard Version, copyright © 1960, 1962, 1963, 1968, 1973, 1975, 1977 The Lockman Foundation.

ESV Study Bible, copyright © 2001, 2008 by Crossway.

**To order additional copies of this study,
visit www.StoneSoupforFive.com or Amazon.com.**

Writing and illustrations: Kari Denker
Editor: Kristen He

Printed in the United States of America

First Printing 2018

Copyright © 2018 Kari Denker

# table of contents

## Philippians 1

- joy in the wait
- growing in love
- joy in prayer
- growing in proper conduct

## Philippians 2

- growing in Christ
- joy in others
- growing in unselfishness
- growing in humility
- growing in your walk
- growing in reverence
- joy in diligence
- Timothy and Epaproditus

## Philippians 3

- joy in the Lord
- growing in discernment
- growing in faith
- joy in simplicity
- joy in suffering
- growing in righteousness
- growing through sanctification

## Philippians 4

- growing in standing firm
- joy in unity
- joy in rejoicing
- joy in obedience
- growing in your thought life
- growing in godliness
- joy in any situation
- joy in giving
- joy in the glory of God

# Welcome to Journal and Doodle through Philippians!

I'm so glad you're here. Let me take a moment to show you around this unique way to study the Bible so you can get the most out of it.

For each chapter of Philippians we'll be studying the themes of growing and joy. It's loosely laid out to do one page a day, but you can do more or less depending on your time… which is why it has checkboxes. Just check off what you've done and pick up where you left off next time!

When we are working through the chapters you'll notice I encourage you to read the chapter multiple times. Though you may be tempted to skip this part, make it a challenge to yourself to do it. After multiple readings you'll start to notice new things, and it will refresh your mind as to where we are and what we are doing. Trust me, it's good for you! Time is precious and these studies are designed to use it well with no busy work.

Speaking of not finding things here, you also will not find fill-in-the-blank questions. This study will guide you through discovering the Word of God and applying it to your life in practical ways. We'll do lots of doodling, list making, and journaling to get the truths of Scripture to sink in and change your heart.

Part of changing your heart is going slowly and diving deeply into the Word of God. You won't find assigned days or times in this study. It's not a 6 week study or a 13 week study. It's a customizable study designed to fit into your life rather than you trying to fit your life around it. You get permission to work on it at your own pace in your own way.

The main requirement for success however, is to have fun and allow yourself to enjoy Bible study. I pray your will enjoy your time with Journal and Doodle through Philippians!

*Kari*

# Gather supplies

I'm so thankful you are here and ready to dig into God's Word in an inductive, creative, and interactive way. I pray this Bible study blesses you! Before we get started here is a quick list of some items you will want to have on hand.

### recommended tools:

Bible (This study was written using the NASB and ESV but you can use whatever version you prefer.)
Dictionary
Sticky notes
Pencil/pens/highlighter
Journal*

*About your journal: Get a journal that is not so fancy that you freeze up when you think of writing in it. My journal is a cheap, staple-bound journal. You can use a sketchbook, a composition notebook, or a spiral bound journal. You will enjoy the study the most if you have a journal approximately the size of a composition notebook. Smaller ones don't give you enough room to do the activities and doodles.

### optional items:

white out tape
colored pencils
sticky notes
concordance
markers
washi tape
stickers

# Philippians journal setup

For the first day or two of your study, we're going to be setting up your journal so you get the most out of your time in this study.

## ☐ table of contents:
Open your journal and decide if you are going to have a table of contents. If you want one in your journal, write the Table of Contents in this Bible study into your journal (or photocopy the page and glue it in), and number the bottom of your journal pages to refer to as you work through each section.

## ☐ summary page:
The next page in your journal will be your summary page. On this page, you will write a very brief summary for each chapter of Philippians. You should only need this one page. Draw a banner or flag at the top and write "summary" on it. Leave it blank for now.

## ☐ overview:
Label the next page in your journal "overview" and give yourself the time to read through the introduction to Philippians in your Bible. If your Bible doesn't have an introduction page, I've listed two below that are free online. Add any thoughts, questions, or information that stands out onto your overview page.

https://www.gty.org/library/bible-introductions/MSB50/philippians
(John MacArthur's introduction to Philippians)
or
https://www.blueletterbible.org/Comm/mhc/Phl/Phl_000.cfm?a=1104001
(Matthew Henry's brief introduction to Philippians)

#JOURNALANDDOODLE

# Author

### Who wrote Philippians?

In order to better understand the book of Philippians, we need to know more about who wrote it and why. First let's look into who Paul, the author, was.

☐ Turn to a new page and title it "Author." Draw a picture of Paul on the page leaving lots of room for notes around him.

☐ Read Philippians 3:4-14. Add what you learn about Paul to your page.

☐ Next, read Acts 22:3-21 and add what Paul says about himself.

### Who were the Philippaians?

☐ Read Acts 16 starting at verse twelve. Take notes on the city, who the Philippians were, and any specific people mentioned.

### Why did Paul write to the Philippians?

☐ What was going on? Paul mentions a few of the reasons in the letter itself. Read Philippians 1:12-14; 2:1-4; 2:19-30, 3:1-2; 4:1-4; and 4:15-18. Write down some of the reasons that Paul wrote to them based on these verses.

Map work:

Next we are going to do some map work so we can get an idea of the location of Philippi and its proximity to other places as well as where Paul was when writing.

☐ At the back of this study guide, there is a copy of a blank map that you can use to either trace into your journal or tear out and glue in onto a page titled "map work."

☐ Turn to the next page in this Bible study guide to find the locations to add to your map.

Some Bible scholars believe this letter to the Philippians was written during Paul's first imprisonment in Rome. There are other scholars who say it might have been written at other locations (Ephesus and/or Caesarea), but to me the evidence seems to stack up that it was probably written while he was in Rome. (Since Rome isn't on the map, I just drew an arrow and labeled it "to Rome.")

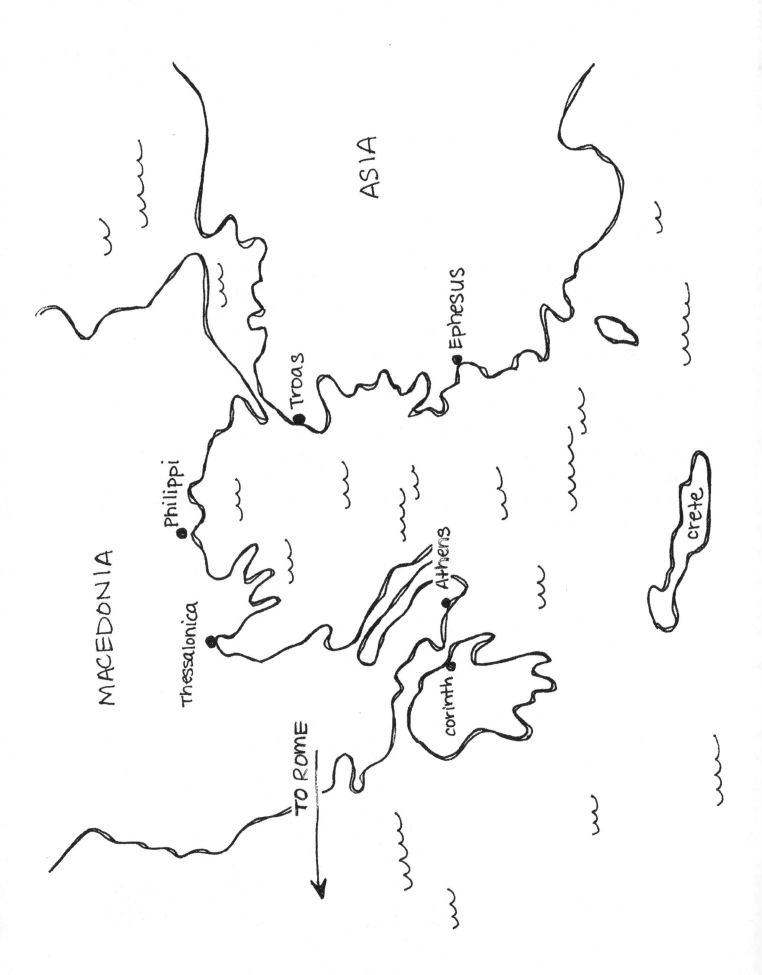

If I have observed anything by experience, it is this; a man may take the measure of his growth and decay in grace according to his thoughts and meditations upon the person of Christ, and the glory of Christ's Kingdom, and of His love.

—John Owen

doodle library

# Philippians 1
## in your journal

- ☐ Title a page in your journal "Philippians One." You might want to write this in a banner or flag or in fancy or fun writing.

- ☐ Pray for God to remove distractions, open your eyes to His truth, and give you wisdom and understanding through His Spirit.

- ☐ Read through chapter one, looking for words and ideas that are repeated. Write these words down on your page next to a key doodle. Title this list "key words." IMPORTANT: For you who think you have to do this "right" and research what other scholars have said are the key words, just stop and take a deep breath. I want you to list repeated words that stand out TO YOU. It's not another pastor's or theologian's key words, but what stands out TO YOU. This is your study, your time in the word. After you finish this guide, knock yourself out with researching more, but for your time right now look for what God is speaking to YOU through His Word.

- ☐ Highlight a verse (or verses) that stands out to you and then write it down on your Philippians one page.

- ☐ Turn to the summary page you created during the introduction, and summarize chapter one in a sentence or even just a few words.

This helps you focus when you read. There is no "right" or "wrong" here and you will not be graded. When I do this, if I find that I cannot summarize the chapter, then I re-read until I can. Focus— it is all about focus. Then test yourself with a summary!

*For I am confident of this very thing, that He who began a good work in you will perfect it until the day of Christ Jesus. —Philippians 1:6*

# Philippians 1
## joy in the wait

☐ Re-read chapter one and title a new journal page "joy in the wait."

☐ Read Philippians 4:10, 14-18 and write them in your journal.

As he was writing this letter, Paul was isolated from most everyone but Roman guards and occasional visitors. He was chained and waiting... and waiting... and waiting... for a trial and possibly an execution. But while he was waiting he was still working to be useful to God and others. Do you think that maybe this was part of the reason he could find joy in writing to the church and even joy in his circumstances? In your journal draw Paul in chains (see example on the next page).

"See how the heart of the apostle is at work: his emotions are not dried up by his personal griefs. He takes a delight in his friends at Philippi; he has a lively recollection of the time when he and Silas were shut up in prison there, and that same night baptized the jailor and his household, and formed the church at Philippi." -C. H. Spurgeon

John Bunyan, the author of Pilgrim's Progress, wrote the first part of his book while in prison. After he was released, he stopped writing and did not finish the book. Perhaps getting back to normal life got in the way or finishing. God had a plan for him, however, and Bunyan was imprisoned a second time. This second imprisonment was when he finished his book. Was he imprisoned each time so he could do the work God had for him?

☐ What about me? What about you? Are we that same way— too distracted to do what God has for us? Are you and I using our freedom and time well? Are we serving Him with what we have, where we are? Take some time to make a list of time-wasters and distractions in your life. then pray for wisdom to limit or remove them

☐ Are you in a waiting time now? Perhaps you are waiting for the Lord to heal you... To change a rebellious child's heart... To bring a husband into your life... To provide a job... To show you what the next step is... What is your wait? And how long has it been? Write it down in your journal.

☐ How has your attitude been during the wait? In your journal draw some "mood faces." (See doodle library.) Which attitude best describes you during the wait? Draw the face then write down what you have been thinking and doing during your waiting time. Have you been on the couch with ice cream and Netflix in misery trying to avoid everyone and everything? (not me!) Have you been running through your head every possible negative outcome? *cough* Or have you been seeking ways to be useful or used by God?

- ☐ Paul's joy shines through in this epistle because he is CONFIDENT. He knows that God is working in his life and other believers' lives. Right now, in your journal, write down some ideas of things you can do to be faithful in your wait, like Paul.

- ☐ Because the wait is usually long and drawn out, sometimes it is hard to imagine it will ever end. We are then tempted to give up or doubt God's goodness to us. Instead of walking that same old route, let's make a plan for beating doubts and worries when they hit. Let's plan what we will do, what verses we will recite, and what we will pray when the wait is long and wearisome.

- ☐ Start with writing out Paul's words in verse six. Are there any other verses you already know that give you confidence in God's faithfulness?
(For example: Jeremiah 29:11, 1 Corinthians 1:9, and 1 Thessalonians 5:24)

- ☐ Joy is confidence in God. And confidence is only gained through knowledge and experience. I do not have to wonder if my writing chair will be safe for me to sit on because I have sat on it and experience it holding me up daily. Confidence in God is the same— it is grown when we experience and know God. How has He worked in the past? How is He working in your life now? Are you actively looking for how He is working now? Are you asking God for wisdom in seeking His will (James 1:5-6)? Answer all these questions in your journal. Make some big long lists if you can! Rejoice in His protection, provision, and faithfulness.

- ☐ Start committing some of the verses on faithfulness to memory. Write them on cards and place them throughout your home. When doubts and worries start to creep in again, recite! (Even if you want to wallow instead. We cannot afford to pamper ourselves and make excuses for ourselves here.)

- ☐ When the worries come, what will you pray? I have written notes and praises to God in my prayer notebook. They remind me of the truth when fear blinds my eyes and worry binds my heart in iron chains. If you have a prayer notebook, add notes of truth and praise to it. Remind yourself constantly.

- ☐ Actively build your love and knowledge of God. Seek to be used by Him. Choose to be confident in the gospel. Choose to be confident that He will perfect His work in you and in all things. Be sure to remember, though, that we are to be waiting on the Lord, not the thing. We are looking to Him, not the situation around us. Amen?

"...what the Lord begins, He will complete, and if He puts His right hand to any work, He will not stop until the work is done, whether it is to strike Pharaoh with plagues, and at last to drown his chivalry in the Red Sea, or to lead His people through the wilderness like sheep, and bring them in the end into the land that flows with milk and honey. In nothing does Jehovah turn from His intent. 'Has He said and shall He not do it? Has He purposed it, and shall it not come to pass?' 'He is God and changes not, and therefore the sons of Jacob are not consumed.'

There is a world of argument in the quiet words which the apostle uses. He is confident, knowing what he does of the character of God, that He who has begun a good work in His saints will perform it until the day of Christ."

—Charles Spurgeon

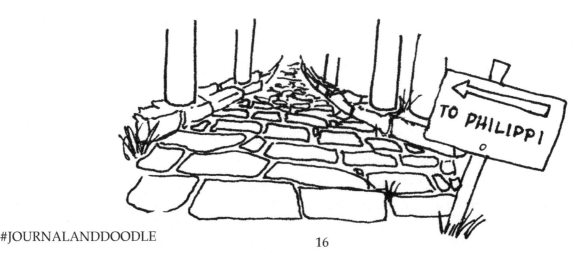

# Philippians 1
## growing in love

☐ Re-read chapter one.

☐ Notice that the Philippians are loving, generous, and thoughtful. Yet in verse nine, Paul prays that their love will abound still more and more. And not only that, but that their abounding love (literally: love upon love) will be in real knowledge and all discernment--not a blind, thoughtless love. Then Paul lists a lovely chain of events and rich results of love and God's work in our lives. Let's list! (I love, love lists!)

☐ For this section we are going to do it a little differently. Start with a fresh two-page spread (you will be working on only the left side page for this part. At the top of the page, write out the first part of verse nine: "that your love may abound still more and more."

☐ Draw two arrows down from that, one pointing slightly left, and the other slightly right. Below one arrow write "real knowledge," and below the other write "all discernment." Note that this is a RESULT of abounding love. God will do it.

☐ Draw an arrow down from under "real knowledge" and write out "that you may approve the things that are excellent." Again, write near here that this is another RESULT of abounding love that God will work in our life.

☐ Draw another arrow down from there and write "sincere and blameless." This is yet another BENEFIT of abounding love that God will work in us.

☐ Draw another arrow down and write out "filled with the fruit of righteousness." Draw a peach or apple near it. Note that this BENEFIT is given THROUGH Jesus.

☐ Now draw the final arrow down to a cloud or starburst with the words "glory and praise of God" written in it. THIS. This is our life purpose. THIS is what our ultimate aim is!

☐ Now for that page over there on the right of your journal. We're going to go a bit more in depth into each of these areas. Draw a big arrow from the verse you wrote at the top across to the right page. End the arrow a bit onto the right side page.

#JOURNALANDDOODLE

# Philippians 1
# growing in love

**agapé**

☐ Before we start looking closer into the words, let's take a step back for a second and look at the context. What is being explained in verses 9-11? Why is Paul explaining it? Write your thoughts in your journal, or on a sticky note (label the sticky note "context") and then put it in your journal.

☐ The word Paul uses for love in verse nine is the Greek word *agape*. (We are talking about the Greek words because the Bible was originally written in Greek, and the Greek vocabulary was much fuller than English.) They had many words for love, so looking closer into which word Paul used sheds more light on the meaning behind it.) A word study on *agape* from preceptaustin.org gives wonderful insight into it: *"Biblical **agape love** is the love of choice, the love of serving with humility, the highest kind of love, the noblest kind of devotion, the love of the will (intentional, a conscious choice) and not motivated by superficial appearance, emotional attraction, or sentimental relationship. **Agape** is not based on pleasant emotions or good feelings that might result from a physical attraction or a familial bond. **Agape** chooses as an act of self-sacrifice to serve the recipient."* Paul is praying this kind of love abounds more and more for them. Love that is a choice of the will, not a feeling or emotion. This applies to our love for others and our love for God. At the end of the arrow you drew over onto this page, write what stands out to you from this definition and any thoughts you have.

☐ Draw two arrows over from the previous page where you wrote "real knowledge and all discernment." (I like to draw curvy arrows, so they can curve under, over, and around other writing.)

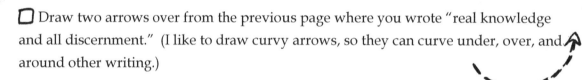

☐ The definition of the word used for "real knowledge" means a knowledge that is based on a personal experience with the object. It is not just reading about it or watching it, but experiencing it and interacting with it. (The difference between reading about hiking across Alaska and actually hiking across Alaska.) A.W. Pink put it this way: *"The world says that "love is blind," but the love of the Christian should be enlightened, well instructed, and directed in all its exercises, effects, and manifestations by the Scriptures."*

☐ This love is not only speaking of love for others, but also of our love for God. We should *experience* it. In order to experience it, we have to be paying attention. We also must invest our time and our energy. There are no short cuts. If we want to abound more and more in our love of God, we need to actually walk, talk, trust, and live life with Him. It is purposeful, intentional, and making time for learning and living. What would that look like in your life right now? Write your thoughts out at the end of your arrow from "real knowledge."

# Philippians 1
## growing in love

☐ "All discernment" comes from three Greek words that mean "delicate spiritual perception." But before we even get to that, look at the word right before this one: "all." The word all in this context means "continually necessary." Discernment must be used *all the time*. Discernment is a sense, an understanding of good and bad, an understanding that things differ. One commentator said, *"Our consciences should become more and more sensitive: we should always be advancing in our discovery of our own evils, and be more conscious of our sins, the fewer we have of them."* At the end of the arrow from "all discernment," write out what this means and what it would look like for you.

☐ Discernment is not only seeing moral problems or sins in others but also in ourselves. We are saved and purified by Christ and His perfect life and death on our behalf, but we are sinners that need to be conformed into the image of Christ. As soon as we are saved, we are *fully* and *completely* in right standing with God. We cannot ever be any more (or less!) righteous—He says so. (If you aren't sure you agree, look up Romans 8:9-11, 2 Corinthians 5:21, Ephesians 4:24 and Philippians 3:9).

It helps me to visualize it like this: When I accepted Christ, His Holy Spirit came to live inside me, which made me alive and gave me a glowing core—like the warp core on *Star Trek Voyager*. I became righteous. I got a beautiful blue glowy-spiraly incredible warp core. I was dead (no warp engines, Captain!); but became instantly alive in Christ. It's not that I was bad and now I'm good. I was dead and now I'm alive. I can't be more alive than I already am. That is who I am at the core, and it will not change.

However, there is clay (which will play the part of sin in our visual illustration) all around the core. It is hard, slow work to remove the clay and let the core show. As we move through our walk with God, He bumps up against that clay and chips and cracks it off so more and more of that righteous core can shine out. Sometimes He does this when we read the Word and the Holy Spirit quietly puts His finger on sin and convicts us. When we allow Him to scrape off sin that way, it hurts— but not as much as when He has to use catastrophic means because we're not listening to Him or we're actively ignoring Him. Sometimes we hold tight to the clay—or even pick up more and slap it on— forming a clay lump that we guard and protect and until God lets us fall on our face and it shatters sending out shrapnel that can hit others and cause them pain too. I am so tired of the hard way. Can you relate? If so, journal about some of your clay-scraping sessions.

☐ Are you striving to know God better and better? Are you allowing the Holy Spirit to scrape away the sins in your life? Is it usually the easy way or the hard way? What do you need to change? Are you praying Paul's prayer for your life?

this is the warp core, the middle is blue and white and glowy.

this is the clay, it's not so beautiful or glowy.

#JOURNALANDDOODLE

# Philippians 1
## joy in prayer

☐ Re-read chapter one, looking for any mentions of prayer or praying and highlight or note them on a new page titled "prayer." Prayer is a major theme in this chapter. Paul prays for the Philippian church and he tells them what he prays. He is absolutely confident that prayer works.

☐ How are you doing in prayer? Journal your thoughts about your current prayer life. Maybe even draw a bar and rate yourself from one to ten, with one being a non-existent prayer life, to ten being Paul's kind of prayer life. Next, write out Philippians 1:4 (pray with joy) and 1:19 (pray with confidence) draw boxes or clouds around them.

☐ On your page, draw three big circles (Big. You are going to be writing in them!). Around the outside of each circle, label one JOY, the other CONFIDENCE, the other CONSISTENCY.

☐ Think of something you've been praying about for a while. Have you been praying with joy? If not, how could you change your prayer to reflect joy and confidence? Write out a prayer in your "joy" circle and include a healthy dose of joy (even if it's not a joyful situation that you are praying about— emulate Paul and seek joy.)

☐ Are you praying with confidence? Are you sure that God will answer (even if it is not what you think you want the answer to be)? How can you better reflect that in your prayer and your actions? Write out the same prayer you did in the joy circle, but in the confidence circle, include confidence that God will work.

☐ Are you praying with consistency? Multiple times and to multiple churches Paul stated that he was *always* praying. That does not mean that he was always on his knees, but rather that he always had a prayerful mindset, a near constant conversation going with God. Do you find that you are constantly distracted during the day? What about during prayer? Do you forget about or not make time to pray regularly and consistently? Do you want to change that? What tiny step could you take today to improve? Journal your thoughts in the circle for consistency.

1 — non-existent prayer life
5 — about average prayer life
10 — prayer life like Paul's #prayerwarrior

#JOURNALANDDOODLE

# growing in proper conduct
*Philippians 1*

☐ Re-read chapter one again. I'm sure you noticed them but mark the recurrence of the words "joy" and "rejoice" and list them on your Philippians one page as key words.

☐ Draw a sign labeled "Proper Conduct" on a new journal page. Paul admonished the Philippians to conduct themselves in a manner worthy of the gospel of Christ (verse 27). He dreaded being put to shame or bringing shame on the name of Christ (verse 20). What does Christian conduct look like according to Paul (verses 27-30)? Write out Paul's words in your journal

☐ What does Christian conduct (worthy of the gospel of Christ) look like for modern believers? Make a list under the sign of all you think of then look to these verses for more: Matthew 7:12, Romans 12:9-21, 1 Corinthians 9:26-27, Philippians 4:9, 1 Thessalonians 5:21-22.

☐ Focusing only on yourself and the sin and struggles in your life (not the sin you see in others' lives), what would proper conduct look like in your life? Think about a specific circumstance, action, or attitude and apply God's truth. Add your thoughts to your journal.

I'll repeat this over and over because I'd much rather risk having you bored of hearing it, than misunderstand this great truth: We are not working for our salvation. It is done. Once we accepted Christ as our Savior, it was finished. We who were **dead** are now **alive**!

The things we read about growing in love, prayer, and proper conduct are not to have God love us or forgive us more or in any way to work our way toward heaven. Instead, this is sanctification — our growth to look more like Christ. We already have our glowing "warp core;" we are in the life-long process of having the clay knocked off. I love this thought from Matthew Henry: *"There is much opposition, and there is need of striving. A man may sleep and go to hell; but he who will go to heaven must look about him and be diligent."* We are not being diligent to get to heaven; we are being diligent to **grow**. We are a work in progress, continually growing in Christ.

Salvation is a gift; sanctification is a duty. We who are saved should have a holy hunger to kill sin, the sin that put our Savior on the cross. And we must be diligent to grow in faith and love in Christ Jesus. (2 Timothy 1:13, 2 Peter 3:18)

Salvation = DONE

Sanctification = DUTY

#JOURNALANDDOODLE

# review and reflect chapter one

☐ Take a few moments (or a day or two!) to review and reflect over all you've learned so far in chapter one. (The great thing about this study is you are not on a timeline. However long it takes to work through this is just fine. There is no race and there is no trophy for finishing first. Lasting change comes from slowing down, spending time thinking, praying, asking the Holy Spirit to guide and change your heart. That takes time, so give yourself the freedom to even take a few days to reflect.)

☐ Look back on the repeated words you listed on the first page for chapter one. Now ask some questions about those words: Why do you think Paul chose those words? What do they mean?

☐ Look back on the list of proper nouns and pronouns referring to people in this chapter. What can you glean about the people it is written to? About Paul? About God? Jesus? What did these people do? What did they see or participate in? What did Paul ask of them?

☐ What did you learn about love in this chapter?

☐ What did you learn about prayer?

Below is a great quote to think and reflect on. Give yourself time to mull it over.

"Where is there an instance of God's beginning any work and leaving it incomplete? Show me for once a world abandoned and thrown aside half-formed! Show me a universe cast off from the Great Potter's wheel, with the design in outline, the clay half hardened, and the form unshapely from incompleteness! Direct me, I pray you, to a star, a sun, a satellite-no, I will challenge you on lower ground-point me out a plant, an ant, a grain of dust that has about it any semblance of incompleteness!" -Charles Spurgeon

#JOURNALANDDOODLE

# notes, quotes, and doodles

"...remember, it is not hasty reading-but serious meditating upon holy and heavenly truths that make them prove sweet and profitable to the soul."
—Thomas Brooks

doodle library

#JOURNALANDDOODLE

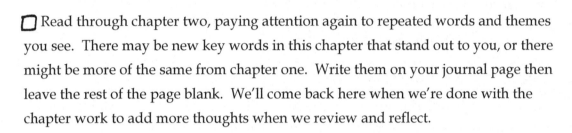

# Philippians 2
## in your journal

☐ Turn to a new page in your journal and title it Philippians Two.

☐ Pray for God to clear your mind and ask the Holy Spirit to guide and teach you.

☐ Read through chapter two, paying attention again to repeated words and themes you see. There may be new key words in this chapter that stand out to you, or there might be more of the same from chapter one. Write them on your journal page then leave the rest of the page blank. We'll come back here when we're done with the chapter work to add more thoughts when we review and reflect.

☐ Highlight a verse (or verses) that stand out to you in your Bible or write them on your Philippians two page in your journal.

☐ Summarize the chapter in a few words on your summary page.

"Humility is not thinking less of yourself,
it's thinking of yourself less."
—C.S. Lewis

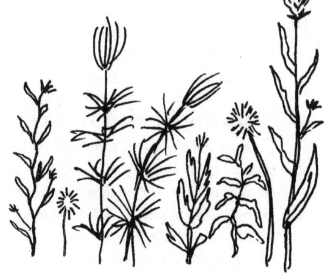

#JOURNALANDDOODLE

# Philippians 2
# growing in Christ

☐ At the top of a new journal page (You might want to make this section a two page spread, so you have lots of room!) write out "IN CHRIST THERE IS..." Now spread out all over the rest of the page and write out the five main headings Paul writes about in verse one. I will list them here:

1. encouragement in Christ
2. consolation of love (or comfort, depending on your Bible translation.)
3. fellowship (or participation) in the Spirit
4. affection
5. compassion (or sympathy/mercy)

☐ Paul is using rhetorical questions, in essence saying we DO have these things in Christ. Under or near each point, write out the definition of the main word of each point. (For example: write out the definition of encouragement, consolation, fellowship, etc.)

☐ Draw brackets or highlight the first three points you listed. Note on your page that these are the result of Christ's work in your *inner* life. You could draw a stick figure of you and an arrow pointing to the heart for these points. Then highlight or bracket the last two points and note that these are a result of Christ's work that shows in your outer behavior.

## encouragement

☐ Draw a cross or Jesus near where you wrote "encouragement in Christ." The Greek word used for encouragement means to call toward, to help, or strengthen and establish. When used of Christ, it means to strengthen and establish a believer's faith. What things about Christ encourage and strengthen you? Is it that He has lived and died for you (1 John 3:5)? That He conquered sin and death (2 Timothy 1:10)? That He controls everything (Hebrews 2:8-10)? That Satan has no power over Him (John 14:30)? That He is God (Titus 2:13)? Write your thoughts, then write down what that encouragement in Christ should look like in your life if you were truly living it out.

## consolation (comfort) of love

☐ Consolation of love is knowing I am loved. It is knowing that everything that happens (good and bad) all comes through the hands of God who knows and loves me. It is true comfort to remember that suffering is only to change the worst of me, not to destroy me. It is true comfort to know that the Spirit, the comforter, is RIGHT HERE, RIGHT NOW. But it is so easy to lose sight of that. This love is for you. Do you know this? Do you live this? How will you embrace this? Journal your thoughts.

# Philippians 2
# growing in Christ

## fellowship (participation) of the Spirit

☐ Do you participate in or have fellowship with the Spirit? (Note that I'm not asking if you HAVE the Spirit — if you are a believer, you do; "warp core" remember? — but I'm asking if you PARTICIPATE or have FELLOWSHIP with the Spirit.) Do you see Him working in your life? In what areas? Do you sense His conviction when you sin? He is your teacher, do you listen to Him as He leads and teaches? Or are your ears and heart clogged up with doubt and/or sin?

☐ What should fellowship with the Spirit look like in a Christian's life? To help here, look up what the Spirit does in John 14:16-17, 26; 16:5-15. Do you allow Him to work like this in your life? Why or why not? Write the good and bad. Include the times where He HAS worked in your life, and the times when you have gotten in the way.

The next two points are the results of Christ's work in your life that are outward and seen by others. Draw another stick figure — this one helping another.

## affection

☐ Do you have affection just toward those you enjoy being around? What about those who are hard to love or work with? (See Philippians 4--the fighting women.) If you struggle here (don't we all?) maybe this will help: It is not "fake it till you make it" but rather a thorough search of your heart and why you struggle. What do you need the Spirit to scrape off to help you love them as Christ does? Spend time praying for God's love to change and shape your heart. Pray, ask, and try again. Lather, rinse, repeat. Over and over.

## compassion (sympathy, mercy)

☐ Do you have compassion, sympathy, and mercy for others? Think of the most compassionate people you know. What do they do? Think about how you show compassion and mercy in your family life. When is it easy to show compassion to those in your family? What times are you most likely to be uncompassionate? What about compassion and mercy to other believers and non-believers? What about compassion to yourself? Journal through each of these areas in your notebook.

One of the best ways to grow in this area is to ask the Lord to open your eyes to the root of the problem in yourself. Ask Him to continue to grow you and mold you and then ask for Him to open your eyes to grow your compassion in every area of your life. Take some time to pray right now.

#JOURNALANDDOODLE

# Philippians 2
## joy in others

☐ Re-read chapter two and underline or highlight words that refer to a proper mindset.

☐ Write verse two in the center of your page and draw tools around the edges.

☐ Write out how Paul says the Philippians can complete his joy. (Hint: I found four points in verse two, which are really one point written from different angles.) The first and last points are all about unity and the two middle points are our work. We need to start and end with the proper mindset (our hearts and desires directed and set on Christ), and we need to do the work. (Thus the tools!)

☐ What is our work? It's to maintain the same love and be united in the same spirit. (I really like the NASB translation here, it is not *have* the same love, but *maintain* the same love.) Relationships always require upkeep. We will, by default, drift apart and become more self-centered through no effort of our own unless we fight to the contrary. (It is just like running, if you do not keep up a regular running routine, you will quickly lose that ability and have to work hard to regain lost ground. Ask me how I know.) Our minds will always default to thinking of ourselves and not of Christ. How can you fight this infuriating natural default of drifting away from Christ? How can you fight drifting away from love for others? Be thoughtful and specific and write down your thoughts to these two questions. I'm not speaking of what Christians in general should do, but what YOU can do in YOUR life right now.

☐ Look up and write out Romans 12:14-18. In fact, here it is from The Voice translation because sometimes hearing familiar verses in a fresh way helps (parenthesis mine):

> "If people mistreat or malign you, bless them. *(That's praying for them!)* Always speak blessings, not curses. *(Not speaking bad of them!)* If some have cause to celebrate, join in the celebration. *(Celebrate, not get jealous!)* And if others are weeping, join in that as well. *(Cry and join in the grief, don't offer to "fix.")* Work toward unity *(Work. WORK toward unity)*, and live in harmony with one another. Avoid thinking you are better than others or wiser than the rest *(take every thought captive!)*; instead embrace common people and ordinary tasks *(nothing and no one is beneath you)*. Do not retaliate with evil, regardless of the evil brought against you. Try to do what is good and right and honorable as agreed upon by all people. If it is within your power, make peace with all people."

☐ Are there any relationships you need to work on? You have the power to do this because you have the Spirit living in you. It requires God scraping off enough of your wants and desires to allow what is already inside to shine out. It is not complicated, but it is definitely not easy. List at least one (or a few) relationships that need priority right now. What will you do? When? Write your thoughts out.

#JOURNALANDDOODLE

# Philippians 2
## growing in unselfishness

☐ Re-read chapter two slowly and thoughtfully.

☐ The first two verses of this chapter were dedicated to encouragement, joy, love, and unity. Now Paul writes why we struggle in these areas: selfishness. Why do you think Paul contrasts selfishness with humility instead of something else like generosity? Just think on that for a bit and we will come back to it.

☐ Turn to a new page in your journal and all around this page, as close to the edge as possible, draw a simple line frame (like the one on the doodle library page). Now, inside that frame, draw another box. See the example. - - - - - - ▷

☐ In the center of the page, inside the second box you drew, write out verses three and four. You can make this take up the whole space, or even do a cool word cloud with it like the Philippians one at the front of the study. Have fun with it, but do not let yourself get locked up on this part. If the word "art" makes you itchy, then just write it out in big letters and that will be great.

☐ Now, inside the blank frame you made, let's do some work. When selfishness rears its head in your life, what does it look like? Take a moment to think about that, then write some words or short thoughts or examples inside that space. You do not have to journal a lot, just think of one or two words that describe your feelings. What triggers selfishness? If you can think of specific instances, you might want to draw some doodles that remind you of those times. For example, on my page I would write (probably in a scribble or dark black bold font): laziness, greed, jealousy, lover of ease and comfort, etc. I remember a time when I had just sat down with a book and a glass of ice water on our back patio on a nice summer day and as soon as I sat down (literally!) my husband asked me if I could run to the store for him to get a pipe fitting. Of course selfishness raged and I sighed, complained, and grumped my way to the store (unfortunately it does not count as serving and blessing your husband if you throw a fit in the process!). So, in remembrance of that lovely moment, I would draw a PVC pipe fitting on my page too.

☐ We are going to continue learning about humility in the next section. If you cannot think of anything to draw or write in your frame right now, it is fine to leave it and come back to it as you think of things.

29 #JOURNALANDDOODLE

## Philippians 2
# growing in humility

☐ Re-read chapter two underlining or circling proper nouns and pronouns.

☐ Turn to a new page in your journal and title it "The Hymn of Christ, or "The Messiah Poem." This is what some Bible scholars call verses five through eleven. It is written as a stirring poem about Christ and His example of how to live a life of humility and unselfishness. You might want to decorate the edge of your page with music notes to represent this "hymn."

☐ Note that this hymn of Christ shows both Christ's divine and human nature, and His humiliation and exaltation. I love this quote from Tim Keller, *"The Christian faith is the only faith that has the total humiliation of God at its center."* Christ is the perfect example of humility and unselfishness.

☐ Paul gives us the weapon to kill selfishness: Humility. It is not giving more so you are less selfish, but rather thinking of yourself less, which is true humility. On your journal page, draw a big cross right in the center. On the cross, write the key words in verses five through eight such as emptied Himself, servant, likeness of men, humbled Himself, etc.

☐ Because of all Christ did in His life and on the cross, write out what God did in verses nine through eleven. You might want to write these out in clouds around the cross and draw some arrows coming out from the cross pointing to them.

☐ Do you display these attitudes of Christ in your life? (We are called to BIG things!) Is there one attitude in particular that you are feeling a nudging or conviction over? If an area is standing out to you, jot down some thoughts about why it is and what you could do to work with the Holy Spirit on scraping away you and revealing more of Christ.

☐ Before we finish up here, read the quote from Puritan pastor Thomas Brooks on the next page, then come back to your journal page and write out anything that stood out to you from that.

☐ What does this teach you about Christ? What does this teach you about yourself?

☐ So back to our question on page 29... why does Paul contrast selfishness with humility? Journal your thoughts based on your work on these pages.

#JOURNALANDDOODLE

# quotable Puritans

[When Satan is telling you that your sins are small, and not really a problem, think on this truth] "...that Christ should come from the eternal bosom of His Father to a region of sorrow and death;

that God should be manifested in the flesh, the Creator made a creature;

that He who was clothed with glory should be wrapped with rags of flesh;

He who filled heaven and earth with His glory should be cradled in a manger;

that the Almighty God should flee from weak man – the God of Israel into Egypt;

that the God of the law should be subject to the law,

the God of the circumcision circumcised,

the God who made the heavens working at Joseph's homely trade;

that He who binds the devils in chains should be tempted;

that He, whose is the world, and the fullness thereof, should hunger and thirst;

that the God of strength should be weary,

the Judge of all flesh condemned,

the God of life put to death;

that He who is one with His Father should cry out of misery, "My God, my God, why have you forsaken Me?" (Matthew 27:46);

that He who had the keys of hell and death at His belt should lie imprisoned in the [tomb] of another, having in His lifetime nowhere to lay His head, nor after death to lay His body;

that the HEAD, before which the angels do cast down their crowns, should be crowned with thorns,

and those EYES, purer than the sun, put out by the darkness of death;

those EARS, which hear nothing but hallelujahs of saints and angels, to hear the blasphemies of the multitude;

that FACE, which was fairer than the sons of men, to be spit on...

that MOUTH and TONGUE, which spoke as never man spoke, accused for blasphemy;

those HANDS, which freely swayed the scepter of heaven, nailed to the cross;

those FEET, 'like unto fine brass,' nailed to the cross for man's sins;

each sense pained with a spear and nails;

His SMELL, with stinking odor, being crucified on Golgotha, the place of skulls;

His TASTE, with vinegar and gall;

His HEARING, with reproaches,

and SIGHT of his mother and disciples bemoaning Him;

His SOUL, comfortless and forsaken;

and all this for those very ["small"] sins that Satan paints and puts fine colors upon."

-Thomas Brooks, <u>Precious Remedies Against Satan's Devices</u>

## Philippians 2
# growing in our walk

☐ Re-read chapter two and note any commands. (I notate commands in my Bible by drawing a check box in front of the verse, just like these here.)

☐ Draw a barbell in the center of a new page. Near that or surrounding it, write out verse 12 and 13 or just the phrase "work out your own salvation."

The first crucial point we need to talk about is "work out your own salvation." Note the context. Paul is talking about humility and Christ's example then tells us "so then... work out your salvation with fear and trembling." It is NOT make your own salvation or get salvation. It is working it out, not working *for*. Your salvation, if you've accepted Christ as your Savior, is DONE. Christ did it ALL. Our responsibility is not to save ourselves through our good deeds; but rather to live lives worthy of the gospel (re-read Philippians 1:27). So then, what does this mean?

One commentator said the phrase "work out" means working thoroughly, taking true pains, being diligent and persevering to the end. It's like working in my yard... I do not enjoy weeding, raking, and fertilizing; so a few times a year I commit to doing yard work because my yard looks bad. But my neighbor's yard across the street? Immaculate. I work on my yard when it gets embarrassing. But my neighbor is out in her yard almost every day. Looking at her yard it is hard to see that she really has anything to do. The weeds she pulls are so tiny that they slip right out of the ground. Mine? Their roots are so healthy and strong they pull up a clod of earth and leave an ankle twisting minefield behind. My neighbor is out there for a half an hour or so almost every day raking, trimming, and cutting flowers. But her work, constant care, and attention to detail make her yard a well-landscaped oasis that is beautiful to gaze at.

☐ How is your spiritual yard? Are you taking pains, working thoroughly, and making diligent use of your time and tools? Or, are you caring for your spiritual life like I care for my yard... waiting until a crisis, a need, or embarrassment drives you to it? Draw some weeds and write out your thoughts in your journal.

☐ List what tools you have available right now to care for your spiritual life. (You could draw more tools like we did on the previous page or some books.) Rate how you are doing in fully using them. Do the same for how you spend (and waste) your time. What does a typical weekday look like for you? What about the weekend? Is there any Sabbath time worked into your week? Is there time for reading and praying? Where and how can you improve?

# Philippians 2
## growing in our walk

☐ We must be cultivators and landscapers, not disaster control and restoration. We must deliberately and intentionally grow in our walk with Christ, because it will NEVER happen by accident. We must not merely read the Bible, but work to apply it to every area of our life. What can you do to make diligent use of the tools and time you have now? (For some of you, there may be precious little time. Working full time, single mothers, or mothers of young ones remember: God does not keep a log of how much time we spend with Him. Rather, He wants us to commune with, talk with, hear from Him, and be changed by His Spirit living in us. Even five minutes is great if that's all you have. Do what you can with the time you have and stay diligent, always watching for ways to grow or moments to redeem. Pray that the Holy Spirit will keep you sensitive to this area of life.)

☐ Brainstorm a list of realistic things you can start to implement to care for your spiritual life with even more diligence.

☐ Choose just one that you could do today and highlight or underline it in your journal. What will you do? When? How?

☐ Remember, it is God who is at work in you. You are not doing this alone. Invite Him to help you and give you the desire to change. You are a new creature in Christ, and the Spirit lives in you! Ask Him to point out areas you need to grow then ask Him to scrape off more of you and convict you in the moment when you are doing anything to the contrary.

☐ On the bottom of your journal page, write out a prayer asking God to help you remember to <u>take pains</u> to work out your salvation. Ask for His help to pull out those weeds, and pray daily for Him to give you a strong, steadfast spirit to persevere.

#JOURNALANDDOODLE

# Philippians 2
# growing in reverence

☐ Re-read chapter two, looking for and circling the words joy and rejoice.

☐ On a new page, draw another barbell and maybe some other workout gear… and write out verse 12. Note we are not to work out anyone else's salvation but our own. Not your husband's. Not your child's. Not your friend's. Not your in-laws'. Not that difficult to get along with Christian. **Your**. **Own**.

☐ Have you tried working out someone else's salvation? In my experience, it has never, ever gone well. Not even slightly. I have PLENTY to do just taking care of my own spiritual life, but oh how tempting it is to be the Holy Spirit in someone else's life! On your journal page, write out 2 Timothy 2:24-26. After writing it out, highlight or color verse 24 and the first part of 25 in pink (where it says what the Lord's bond-servant is to do and not do). Now, highlight the rest of verse 25 and all of 26 yellow. The yellow is God's job. Re-read your job (the pink) again. Re-read God's job (the yellow). I have this verse written out and highlighted on a card by my kitchen window to remind me which job belongs to me. How often I want to do God's job in other people's lives! (It certainly does seem easier to do sometimes, right?)

☐ The definition of fear in verse 12 is not fright but rather "behavior coupled with reverence and respect." (Write that down in your journal.) Remember this is not talking about fear of losing our salvation, but a very real awareness that we will all (with 100% certainty) be called before the throne and asked to give an account of our lives (Romans 14:12). The idea is one of remembering who you are, who God is, and who you would be without Him. It is continually growing in respect for God and remembering what He has done. Take a moment to write out what God has done in your life. What changes has He made? What things has He done? What blessings has He given?

☐ Equally as interesting is the definition from Thayer's Greek Lexicon of trembling (write this one down too!): *"One who distrusts his ability to completely meet all requirements but religiously does his utmost to fulfill his duty."* We cannot save ourselves. We could never do enough. We cannot even live a day (or hour) without the Spirit who is at work in us. Our Christian walk is never a case of gritting our teeth and plodding along, but it is continuing to allow Him to remove enough of our selfish wants and desires and change us to be more like Christ.

#JOURNALANDDOODLE

## Philippians 2
## growing in reverence

Again, allow me to throw out some Puritan thoughts here from Matthew Henry (it's going to hurt, sorry...).

"Secure the welfare of your soul--whatever becomes of other things...trembling for fear lest you miscarry and come short. Be careful to do everything...in the best manner and fear that because of [all our comforts and conveniences and freedoms] we should fall short."

(Ouch. Ouch. Ouch!)

☐ Re-write that in your journal. Bonus points if you personalize it. We have a job to do because He did a greater job for us. We can only carry out our job if we are utterly dependent on His power and His grace.

☐ Use the rest of your page to ask and answer these questions:

☐ What are some of the comforts, conveniences, and freedoms that you struggle with enjoying wisely or often overindulge in?

☐ Which of them take up time and distract to no real usefulness — or even worse — to your detriment?

☐ When and how specifically will you fight against it?

☐ How does being aware of what Christ has done and what is to come in eternity increase your reverence for God and help you in your Christian walk?

☐ End this page with a prayer based on your journal notes.

# Philippians 2
## joy in diligence

☐ Re-read chapter two and underline the words work, toil, and serve (or service).

☐ On a new journal page in the center write out verse 14 then briefly review all you have done so far in your journal.

The context of verse 14 is because of ALL that you have been studying so far. We are called to do all of these things without grumbling and disputing. And as much as I love sharing this verse with my boys who hate to sweep the floor or pick up their smelly rooms—it is really written to ME and MY life and MY working out MY OWN salvation. I am to do all things without grumbling or disputing (disputing here can also be translated as questioning). It is to be my attitude here on earth, but even more, my attitude toward God.

Some of those things that I am to do without grumbling or disputing are my duties as a daughter of God, a wife, and mom. I also have duties as a writer, sister, aunt, friend, teacher, etc. In those areas I am called to have cheerful obedience to the commands of God. (Ouch.)

☐ In your journal, draw a big tree that takes up most of your page. What are God's commands to you? What are your branches of duty? On the trunk write "my duties." In the leafy top part of your tree, write out some of your God given duties. Which duties do you need to prune or organize or tidy up so they are stronger and work better for you? What would pruning these look like in your life?

Here's a bit more Matthew Henry for you (I know, I know, he's so painful but so good!): *"Do it and do not find fault. Mind your work and do not quarrel with it."* Or how about this nugget? *"God's commands were given to be obeyed, not disputed."*

☐ What commands of God do you KNOW He has given you for some of those duties you listed? If you're not sure, start with these verses: 2 Timothy 2:24-25; 1 John 2:15; 1 John 3:18; 2 Peter 1:5-8; James 1:19-20; Titus 2:3-5. Add in any more you can think of.

☐ Journal your thoughts near the tree you drew. Are you doing those duties? Why or why not? Don't make excuses, don't pamper yourself.

# joy in diligence
### Philippians 2

☐ Now you might be feeling all down and discouraged after that and if so, you are missing the point of working out. If you are new or inexperienced at the gym, and you are unable to bench press the same weight that someone else (who has been diligently working out for years) can, do you beat yourself up and head home? We are only able to work out our salvation because of Him who GAVE us that privilege. It is God who is at work in us and His Spirit that even gives us the desire to change. Take a moment here to praise Him that He is faithful and able to work in you and change you, right where you are, at this exact stage of life.

☐ Let's change our focus back to the truth—the promised result! There are both outward results (blameless) and inner results (sincere). And remember that this is not gritting your teeth and pushing through, but relying on the power, love, and self-discipline that you already have through the Spirit! (2 Timothy 1:7) God keeps scraping away that clay, doesn't He?

☐ In your journal write out some more results we're promised:
- We will shine as a light (Matthew 5, Daniel 12:3)
- We will hold fast to the word of life (John 1)
- We are not left alone to figure it all out (Titus 2:11-13)

☐ Can you think of more? Add them in your journal.

☐ Now think through each of those points above. What could each result look like in your life? Give yourself permission to dream… these could be your #goals. What would it look like to shine as light? Hold fast to the word? etc. Work through each area and dream.

☐ End this page with a prayer based on your study so far.

#goals

# Philippians 2
# Timothy and Epaphroditus

☐ Draw two bowling pin men to represent Timothy and Epaphroditus.

☐ Turn to a new page in your journal and read Philippians 4:18 about Epaphroditus.

*"Epaphroditus was the delegate of the Christian community at Philippi, sent with their gift to Paul during his first Roman imprisonment. Paul calls him 'my brother and fellow-worker and fellow-soldier.' The three words are arranged in an ascending scale: common sympathy, common work, common danger and toil and suffering."* -Lightfoot

*"On his arrival at Rome, Epaphroditus devoted himself to 'the work of Christ,' both as Paul's attendant and as his assistant in missionary work. So assiduously did he labor that he lost his health, and 'was sick nigh unto death.' He recovered, however, and Paul sent him back to Philippi with this letter to quiet the alarm of his friends, who had heard of his serious illness. Paul besought for him that the church should receive him with joy and hold him in honor."*
-S.F. Hunter

☐ We have a lot more information on Timothy. Paul wrote two letters to Timothy (1 and 2 Timothy). You can read about his mother and grandmother in 1 Timothy 1:5, and in Acts 16:1-13.

☐ Read Philippians 2:19-30 and write out what Paul says about Timothy there.

☐ Paul gave Timothy good instructions to live by. Look them up and write them down (1 Timothy 4:7-16). We see Timothy as Paul's companion for some missionary journeys and after his journeys with Paul, we see him again in Philippians 1:1 and hear more about him in Hebrews 13:23. Take notes on all you find in these verses about Timothy.

According to tradition, after Paul's death Timothy settled in Ephesus to live and work and there died a martyr's death.

☐ Are there any examples from either man that you could follow? Journal your thoughts.

#JOURNALANDDOODLE

Add to your believing,
deeds that prove it true—
Knowing Christ as Savior,
make Him Master too:
Follow in His footsteps,
go where He has trod,
In the world's great trouble,
risk yourself for God.

—Brian Jeffrey Leech

# review and reflect chapter two

☐ Take a few moments or a day or two to review and reflect over all you've learned so far in chapter two. Remember, there is no rush. Review and reflect and pray. Write your reflections and thoughts on the page you titled "Philippians Two" at the beginning of your work for this chapter. Reflection is where things start to stick, so take your time so things can get sticky!

☐ Look back on the words you wrote down that refer to a proper mindset (page 17 of this study guide). I underlined these words (from the NASB): same mind, united, humility, looking to the interests of others, emptied Himself, humbled Himself, obedient, fear, trembling. Yours might be different according to the translation you used. Look up a one or two definitions for words that stand out to you then write out a few thoughts on how you can work to develop these more in your life.

☐ Look back on the proper nouns and pronouns referring to people in this chapter (page 30). What can you glean about these people? About Paul? What did they do? What did they see or participate in? What did Paul ask of them?

☐ What commands do you see? Make a list of commands and ideas you have to work on obeying them (with help of the Holy Spirit's power.)

☐ What did you learn about joy and rejoicing?

☐ What did you learn about toil, work, and service?

☐ What did you learn about God/Jesus/the Holy Spirit?

# notes, quotes, and doodles

I cannot know Jesus through another person's acquaintance with Him. No, I must know him myself; I must know Him on my own account.
—C. H. Spurgeon

# Philippians 3
## in your Bible

☐ Turn to a new page in your journal and title it Philippians Three.

☐ Pray for God to clear your mind and ask the Holy Spirit to guide and teach you.

☐ Read through chapter three, paying attention again to repeated words and themes. There may be new repeated words in this chapter that stand out to you, or there might be more of the same from chapters one and two. Write them on your journal page then leave the rest of the page blank. We'll come back here when we're done with the chapter work to add more thoughts when we review and reflect.

☐ Highlight a verse (or verses) that stand out to you in your Bible or write them in your journal.

☐ Summarize the chapter in a few words on your summary page.

#JOURNALANDDOODLE

Philippians 3

# joy in the Lord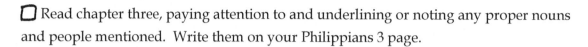

☐ Read chapter three, paying attention to and underlining or noting any proper nouns and people mentioned. Write them on your Philippians 3 page.

☐ Title a new page in your journal "joy in the Lord." Chapter three starts with Paul saying that finally, after all he has written, we are to rejoice in the Lord.

☐ Draw a trumpet and write "rejoice in the Lord" coming from it.

Notice that we are told to rejoice *in the Lord*. This is a phrase most Christians know, but what does rejoicing *in the Lord* really look like in your day to day life? I like what Charles Spurgeon says about this verse: *"Let this be the end of everything; before you get to the end of it, and when you do get to the end of it, 'rejoice in the Lord.' It is incumbent upon us, as Christians, to rise out of our despondencies. Joy should be the normal state of the Christian. But never… come to an end of it. Rejoice in the Lord, and yet again rejoice, and yet again rejoice; and as long as you live, rejoice in the Lord."*

You guys, this prize we have in Christ is worth rejoicing in! It can NEVER be taken away from us! I often lose sight of this and take this precious, precious gift for granted. We are called to repeatedly, always, constantly rejoice in the Lord.

☐ In your journal, make a list of all the things we can rejoice in the Lord about. Remember, it is not rejoicing in earthly or material things, but *in the Lord*. I'll start the list, then you continue:

- Christ saved me. (He chose me, sinful as I am, to be HIS.)
- Christ came to serve. (He is a King who isn't aloof, but servant to all.)
- He destroyed Satan's agenda.
- He gives me power over sin. (I am not enslaved to sin anymore, with His indwelling Spirit I can overcome. Nothing is impossible.)
- He is patient towards me. (He bears with me, loves me, forgives me.)

☐ Now you continue taking stock of your joy, list all the things you can rejoice over in the Lord.

☐ End your time rejoicing to the Lord in prayer and praise.

#JOURNALANDDOODLE

# growing in discernment
## Philippians 3

☐ Reread the chapter and write out any commands on your Philippians Three page.

☐ Paul warns us to beware of dogs, evil workers or mutilators of the flesh. Across the top of your page, draw some barbed wire and a sign that says "beware of dogs." Or if you're feeling extra creative, draw a rabid looking dog. (Remember, dogs in Paul's time weren't household pets. They were wild--more like wolves than Golden Retrievers.)

The Greek word for "beware" meant to mark, to observe, and to be on guard against something. The dogs and evil workers refer to teachings or people who are against Christ and barking and biting and burying people in confusion or misleading them. It could also include teachings and people that are morally upright and good enough to keep from trouble, but who can never be righteous enough to get into heaven (remember, NONE of us are righteous enough to get into heaven or can ever do enough. It's ALL on Christ and His perfect life lived on earth and His sacrifice to give that perfection and righteousness to us!) These moral dogs also confuse, bark, and bite. Both are equally dangerous. We will have a hard time discerning and being wary of the dogs and evil workers if we don't know the truth found in the Bible.

☐ What are some modern-day examples of dogs and evil workers? Write out a list under your heading of "beware of dogs." What have they said that has confused or threatened to mislead you before? Include those points too. God and His Word can stand up to scrutiny and your search for truth.

☐ How can you beware of (mark, observe, and be on guard against) modern day dogs and evil workers? Write out some ideas.

One thing I have been tempted to do in the past is study the evil workers, cults, or false religions. But that is a mistake. I don't need to study their false claims (confusing and filling my head with error) but instead I need to study the Word of Truth: the Bible. If I know the truth, it truly will set me free from the confusion and misleading of false teachings. How are you doing here? Are you spending quality time in the Word of God for yourself? Are you digging out understanding and application? Do not rely on your Pastor, your Bible study guides—or me— to teach you truth. Seek truth out, hunt for it, and pray for a passion for studying and learning His word.

#JOURNALANDDOODLE

# Philippians 3
# growing in faith

☐ Re-read chapter three and turn to a new page in your journal.

In verse one, Paul states that it is no trouble to write the same things over and over again and it is a safeguard for us. I love how Charles Spurgeon puts it: "*...everyone knows, who has ever looked upon the sea, or upon the Falls of Niagara, that look as often as you may, though you see precisely the same object, yet there are new tints, new motions of the waves, and new flashes of the light which forbid the least approach of monotony, and give to the assembling of the waters an ever-enduring charm. Even thus is it with that sea of all delights which is found in the dear lover of our souls!*" We can never plumb the depths of Scripture. We should always keep returning to be refreshed.

Continuing on his theme of rejoicing in the Lord, Paul gives an example from his own life. He had every reason to put hope in his Jewish heritage and elite education. He was one of the most highly educated men of his time. But he gathered all that up and threw it all away. He did it because he found something better than all of that put together: Christ.

☐ We've all been there. We've all been tempted to put our faith in things other than God. What things have tempted you? Was it material things? (A big savings account? A nice house?) Or maybe it was earthly, temporal things. (A good marriage? Great kids? Good health?) Or perhaps it was even spiritual things that you thought might increase your favor with God. (A "no-fail" Bible reading plan? An immaculate church attendance record?). Make a list of anything you've been tempted to put your faith in.

Here's a great quote on this subject from Pastor John MacArthur: "*You know what [Paul] had spent his whole life doing? Doing what he says in the first half of verse nine, trying to gain a righteousness of his own derived from the law. That's what he spent his whole life doing, that's why he was a Pharisee. He was one of the elite 6,000 Pharisees, small number, who believed they could attain salvation by perfect adherence to the law of God. What a burden, what an unbelievable burden, what a guilt trip, what a deception. And he said, 'I give it all up, I'll give all that stuff of having a righteousness of my own derived from the law up gladly.' What kind of righteousness is that? It's the righteousness of self-control...the righteousness of external morality, the righteousness of religious ritual and ceremony, the righteousness of good works, it's self-righteousness. It's the righteousness produced by the flesh.*"

☐ Did you read that last part of the quote? Go back and re-read the last three sentences. Which of these kinds of righteousness have you been tempted to put your faith and hope in? After you've made your list, spend some time journaling. Has the Lord taken any of these things from your life? Are you struggling in one of these areas? Is the Lord teaching you to walk by faith by removing or adding to your life more than you can handle? Is it time to let Him handle it? What would that look like? What do you need to do?

# Philippians 3
## joy in simplicity

☐ As we saw, Paul took all his pedigree, all his law and rule following and wadded it up and threw it away. He simplified everything down to Christ.

I often struggle with joy (believe me, writing these studies is a painful process because I'm writing to myself). I am happy when things are easy, the weather is perfect, the boys are behaved, the bank account has some money left after bills, and I can do what I want for a few minutes each day. But to get to that state, I have to push through the hard stuff and that is often (usually) joyless. We all have work to do, we all have to get hard things done, but Paul is showing us that there is a way to do it *and* have joy in it. (He's writing this while in chains. With joy.) I need joy and it is found only in Christ. When I lose sight of where my joy rests, it is almost always because I've lost the simplicity needed in my life.

I am at my most joyless when I am overwhelmed. And I'm usually overwhelmed because either I'm behind on things, or I'm trying to do too many things. Both of those problems boil down to my "no's." Either I haven't said no to myself (No, Kari, it's not time to surf the internet or check Instagram) or I haven't said no to other things (I can't do ALL THE THINGS. I cannot continue to say YES without first counting what this "yes" going to make me say "no" to.)

☐ On a new journal page draw a cross or Jesus at the center of your page. All around your doodle write out some things that overwhelm you or distract you or clutter your life. Draw clouds around them (probably black clouds).

☐ Now go back and write in things that you know increase your joy in Christ. The titles on most of the pages in this study are all things to help build our growth and joy, so list those too. Draw starbursts around these things.

☐ Highlight or star the items that you feel you really need to cultivate in this season of life. Cross out or darken the edges of the black clouds that you'd really like to eliminate. (We really don't need to read another book or Bible study on joy, we already know what we need to do, we just need to DO IT! )

☐ Take a few minutes to brainstorm what you need to do to grow in joy. Don't skip or just think about this part. Write down some practical ideas.

☐ End your time talking to God and asking for His help and wisdom.

#JOURNALANDDOODLE

## Philippians 3
# joy in suffering

☐ Turn to a new page in your journal and re-read chapter three.

☐ In verse 8 Paul writes his goal in life. On your journal page doodle a finish line banner and write "Paul's main goals." Paul states them in verses 8-10. Under your banner write them out.

That is quite the list! If I were writing that I'd definitely leave off those last two as my life goals. But Paul knows the truth of a life committed to Christ. And, honestly, suffering makes for a good story. How many of us roll our eyes at #blessed Instagram photos of perfectly staged expensive lattes, smiling put together moms cooking with their non-screaming toddler in a gourmet kitchen, or spa-like bathrooms that probably smell faintly of bleach and a tropical island? But in reality a true #blessed life is going to include suffering and hanging on to Christ. THAT is a good story. THAT is a life worth living. (A fun doodle here would be a newspaper with the headline "Sufferings make a story worth telling.")

☐ We are guaranteed to suffer and we need to prepare for it. It's a promise. Look up and write out John 15:20, Acts 14:22, 2 Timothy 3:12, 1 Peter 4:12.

☐ How does Paul set an example for us? In your journal make a heading on drawing of a worn out piece of wood. On it you could write something like Paul's Example, under that list what Paul did to prepare for suffering.

- He recalled his past and the things he valued, and counted them as loss (verses 5-7).
- He thought of his present and counted all things as loss (verse 8).
- He focused on his future and the true prize--knowing Christ Jesus (verses 8b-10).

Notice that it is not a longing loss. It's a loss comparable to throwing out something broken or rotten. He throws away ALL so he may gain Christ. (Note, Paul is not saying to GET Christ, because if you are a believer you already have Christ, but Paul knew very well that valuing things more than Christ would decrease fellowship with Christ, hinder his walk, confuse, mislead, and make him ineffective—losing, not gaining.)

☐ Now you do the same. Think through your past, present, and future. Journal your thoughts on past things that you once valued that really didn't make a bit of difference in the scheme of things. Then think of your present and what things that you value now that you should count as loss. And then focus on your future, and your true prize at the end of it all: knowing Christ. Write it all down in your journal.

☐ What does this teach you about God? What does it show you about yourself? What needs to change?

# Philippians 3
# growing in righteousness

☐ Turn to a new page in your journal and re-read chapter three.

☐ Draw two sign posts, one with a sign that says "do" and another that says "don't." Under those, write out the end of verse eight and all of verse nine. This is a crucial clarifying point about the truth in verse eight.

☐ We have no righteousness of our own created from following the law (or man-made rules of do's and don'ts). Our righteousness is solely based on faith in Christ. Our righteousness comes from God. Not us, not our works, not our abstaining from or doing things. Salvation does not require us to do good works to get it or to maintain it. Look up and write out Romans 8:1, 1 Corinthians 1:30, 2 Corinthians 5:21 under your sign posts. Any good things we do are a result of His completed work in our life. If you hear or read anything different, it is not the gospel of Jesus Christ.

☐ Under those verses draw Jesus. Draw a banner across or above Him and write "righteousness" on it and maybe even starbursts coming from Christ, covering the do's and don'ts above.

☑ Faith in Christ

☐ Draw some arrows pointing to Jesus and write "through faith in Christ." If there are any "to-do's" in our faith, it is this one. Faith in Christ. That's it.

☐ Righteousness comes from God (verse nine) on the basis of faith. You might want to draw some arrows to indicate this on your page. It doesn't come from us at all—it's not us. And it's not us AND God. It's God (His work) on the basis of faith (our job).

☐ Paul goes right from that deep, crucial truth to say what his life goal is in verse ten which we covered earlier. He writes the result in verse eleven. Draw a divider across your page and under that write verses eleven and twelve.

☐ On the bottom corner of your page, draw a goal post. Draw a long path in front of the goal across the bottom of your page and on that path, write out the verbs or actions in verses twelve through fourteen.

☐ What does your work on this section teach you about God?

☐ What does it show you about yourself? Are there any changes you need to make in your life? Any thoughts you need to take captive? Any truths to rest in? Journal your thoughts and end in prayer.

# Philippians 3
# growing through sanctification

The process of sanctification is one of growing and being changed to look more and more like Christ. While we are never going to be perfect on earth (Philippians 3:12) God expects us to continue to grow and change to look more like our Savior.

☐ Mentally divide your page in half, top and bottom. In the center of the top half, draw a sign just the words "press on" (or "follow after" if you're in the KJV). Then in the same top section of your page, write out verses 12-14.

The key term to focus on is "press on." Paul states it twice (verses 12 and 14). The first time he says to press on for our own good. He wanted to "lay hold of that for which also I was laid hold of by Christ." To be honest, this was a bit confusing for me to think about, almost like a riddle. What was the "that" that Christ "laid hold of him?"

☐ The Greek word for "lay hold of" is *katalambano* which means to seize, to take, to apprehend, to catch unawares (write that in your journal). So rewording it helps a bit. "...I press on in order that I may seize that for which I was also seized by Christ."

So why did Christ seize or take hold of Paul? Why did He seize and take hold of me? of you? David Guzik had great insight here: *"Jesus laid hold of Paul to make him a new man (Romans 6:4), so Paul laid hold of that and wanted to see the converting work of Jesus completely carried out in himself. Jesus laid hold of Paul to conform him into the image of Christ Jesus (Romans 8:29), so Paul laid hold of that and wanted to see the nature of Jesus within himself..."*

☐ In light of that explanation why did Jesus lay hold of you? Those same things apply to Paul and us. We need to lay hold of and press on and eagerly look for how Jesus is transforming and conforming us into His image. What in your life that is more in line with the nature of Jesus? What is not? What parts of that clay are you eager to have scraped off? Jot it down in your journal. Write your thoughts in your journal.

☐ Expect and eagerly look for change in your heart that is the work of the Spirit. Have great expectations of the promise of new life, the fruit of the Spirit, God's goodness, mercy, and grace. He saved us not because of anything we have done, but because of His own mercy and grace. Look for that! Have you seen changes from how you used to behave, speak, and think? Think about then write down the ways you've seen His faithfulness to you.

☐ God also saved us to make disciples and to teach others about Him. (Matthew 28:18-20) Are you laying hold of that? Are you allowing the Spirit to work in your life in this way? Ponder that for a moment then move on to the next page.

# growing through sanctification

Philippians 3

- ☐ The next "press on" in verse 14 is urging us to strive toward the goal. What is Paul's goal (verse 14)? He states it then lists how he can press on toward that goal by having the attitude of Christ (verse 15); living to a righteous standard (verse 16); setting a pattern and example (verse 17); teaching truth (verse 18); and looking forward to heaven (verse 21). Write this out on your page.

That is a pretty amazing goal. The prize of the upward call of God is amazing, but also terrifying if not for the second part: "in Christ Jesus." Without Christ, that upward call is the worst thing that can happen. Without Christ, we are telling God our filthy rags are good enough and His standards are too hard or ridiculously wrong. But being "in Christ" means we are covered in His righteousness, covered in His sacrifice, and all our sins were taken away by His work on the cross. We are cleaned, purified, and given the righteous life He lived on our behalf. What a prize!

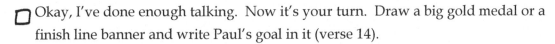

- ☐ Okay, I've done enough talking. Now it's your turn. Draw a big gold medal or a finish line banner and write Paul's goal in it (verse 14).

- ☐ Journal about how you can make Paul's goal your goal and how you can press on just like Paul states in verses 15-21. Personalize each verse and make it very specific to your current season of life. For example, I wrote "I need to remember the end goal isn't getting the boys out of the house with a successful career or retiring with my husband in comfort, security, and ease. My goal is to parent for and live for eternity. I need to have the attitude of Christ Jesus who came and lived in submission, obedience, and love. (Ouch!) Never seeking His own will (Ouch!), but always looking to the Father and His will. (Ouch!)

- ☐ After you work through those verses, write out what that would look like in your life. Referring back to verse 15, I wrote "I need to be less caught up in the day to day grind and distractions, and SEEK OUT teachable moments. I need to prioritize the Word in my life, so I can use it when teaching and sharing with my boys and others. I must be aware of time and how fleeting it is and be diligent to use it wisely, looking forward to and preparing for the upward call of God in Christ Jesus. Rather than the comfort of this world.

- ☐ After this have fun and fill in your page with gold medals or draw trophies.

"Remember this; that your life is short, your duties many, your assistance great and your reward sure: therefore faint not, hold on and hold up in ways of well doing, and heaven shall make amends for all!" -Thomas Brooks

# review and reflect chapter three

☐ Take a few moments (or a day or two) to review and reflect and pray over all you've learned in chapter three.  Make it sticky!

☐ What stood out to you?  What really convicted you?  Write your reflections and thoughts on the page you titled "Philippians Three" at the beginning of your work for this chapter.

☐ Did you learn anything about the people mentioned?  What about Paul?

☐ What do the commands teach you?

☐ What did you learn about pressing on?

# notes, quotes, and doodles

#JOURNALANDDOODLE

# Philippians 4
## in your Bible

- ☐ Pray before you begin.
- ☐ Read through chapter four.
- ☐ Highlight a verse (or verses) that stand out to you in your Bible or write them in your journal.
- ☐ Summarize the chapter in a few words on your summary page.

"To stand fast in the Lord is to stand fast in His strength and by His grace; not trusting in ourselves, and disclaiming any sufficiency of our own."
—Matthew Henry

#JOURNALANDDOODLE

# Philippians 4
## growing in standing firm

☐ Turn to a new page in your journal and re-read chapter four.

☐ What is the context of the first verse in chapter four? What came right before? Re-read the end of chapter three, reviewing what Paul was just talking about and write a couple notes of context.

☐ The church in Philippi was Paul's crown and joy! The Greek word used for crown is *stephanos*, a wreath of honor presented to athletes who win their competition. Draw a laurel wreath in your journal, leaving enough room in the center to write out verse one. The *stephanos* was an elite wreath that represented a lot of discipline and hard work. Paul called the Philippians his crown, his *stephanos*. What does this tell you about Paul and his work there? What does it tell you about the Philippians?

☐ On your page, near the bottom, draw a simple lighthouse and write out the Greek word for stand fast—*steko*, and the definition: to be stationary, to stand firm, to persevere. Nothing stands firm like a lighthouse, designed to stay steady in the fiercest of storms.

☐ Paul urges the Philippians to stand firm because they, like us, are in a tough culture. But notice that it's not stand firm in a grit your teeth and deal with it kind of way, but stand firm IN THE LORD. To stand firm in the Lord is to walk steadily with Him, to be close with Him in prayer and thought, to stand in His love and His grace. Earlier he wrote about people who were enemies of the cross of Christ, and "dogs" who bite and mislead, and people who preach Christ out of selfish ambition. Yet in spite of all this he was telling them "stand firm, remain steady in the Lord" because they have hope! Why do you think Paul reminded the Philippians of this? Do you need this reminder today? Can I get an amen?

☐ What are some of the storms you are facing right now? Write a few words about it near your lighthouse (maybe add some dark clouds and big waves across the bottom of the page if you're feeling creative). How can you stand firm IN THE LORD through these trials? Write out some ideas of what it would look like to walk steadily with Him, to remain close, and to stand in His love and grace in one of the specific situations you are facing right now.

☐ Tim Keller said the opposite of joy is not sadness but hopelessness. Review what our hope is by writing verses 3:20-21 near your lighthouse. How does knowing this truth of what is to come help you find your footing and brace yourself to be firm and consistent and steady in the Lord with joy? Write your thoughts in your journal.

# Philippians 4
## joy in unity

☐ Turn to a new page in your journal and re-read chapter four.

☐ Oh, the fighting women. Draw two fighting or angry women in your journal and write out verses 2 and 3. Maybe they were disagreeing with each other, or maybe they were disagreeing with the church or their family, or their kids... whatever it was that set them off, Paul implores them to be of the same mind. They worked with him, struggling as he had for the gospel and they were precious to him. It is interesting to note, however, that Paul offered no counsel other than to be of the same mind. He didn't fix the problem, offer tools, or any solutions other than unity! He urged others to help them, to join with them, strengthen their hands, encourage them, counsel them. Then he asked others, Clement and the "true companion," to help them.

☐ Are there some believers in your life that you are struggling or clashing with? As far as it depends on you, are YOU working to be at peace with them (Romans 12:18)? Are you working to be unified at least in what you have in common? I'm not talking about a "fake it till you make it" kind of attitude, but truly thinking about what you have in common (Jesus Christ and Him crucified!) and unifying around that? We know we can't change them, but there are some steps we can take that will lead to unity? Sometimes it helps to think carefully through the issues that cause problems. (And, if you're like me, you might e thinking that this relationship may never be a close one, and maybe that is true, but let's agree to have greater expectations of God than we do of our problems.) Work through the following questions in your journal.

☐ Think of the person (or persons!) you are struggling having unity with. You don't need to write their names down (maybe just their first initial?).

☐ List what you have in common with them. Anything and everything.

☐ Are you praying for them? How specifically can you pray for them?

☐ How can you be praying for yourself in this relationship?

☐ Think ahead to this relationship healing or being one of unity. How would it bring joy to your life? How would you feel? How would you act?

☐ What can you do to work toward harmony and unity in this relationship?

☐ Take some time right now to pray for this person and your relationship. Ask the Holy Spirit to do His work in *your* heart to change and mold it to be more like that of

# Philippians 4
## joy in rejoicing

☐ Turn to a new page in your journal and re-read chapter four.

☐ Write out the first part of verse four, "rejoice in the Lord always," across the top of a new page. Write it big enough that it stretches from one side of the page to the other, but keep it on one line. Draw a banner around it or a trumpet by it.

☐ Directly under the word rejoice, write out the definition of rejoice (using either a regular dictionary or BlueLetterBible.com.)

☐ Beneath that, write the definition out in your own words.

☐ Under the words "in the Lord," do the same thing (write the definition and write it again in your own words). What does this mean? Look back in your notes (page 56) if you need help. Write out your thoughts in your journal under the words. (A definition I found for the word "in" was interesting; it denoted a fixed position, quickly, wholly, speedily.)

☐ And finally do the same for the word "always." Write out the definition and then write it out in your own words.

☐ Are you wondering the same thing I am? How can Paul command us to rejoice? How does that work? "Well Paul said I'm supposed to rejoice, so even though this stinks, yay. I'm happy." I don't think so. What if it's more about cultivating and growing a mindset of rejoicing by retraining your focus. Re-read 3:20-21, then turn to 2:5-13 and re-read. This is *true* joy. This is where we need to focus when life starts swirling out of control (again and again).

My focus is either on me or God. (I might try to fool myself that sometimes my focus is on others, but when it comes in the form of worry or anger or frustration it reveals that really my focus is on me. My worry over if something happens or doesn't happen usually means I'm thinking about how will that affect or hurt or disappoint me.) In order to rejoice, my focus MUST be on Him and Him alone.

☐ Yes, that's great, but HOW? Charles Spurgeon said to cultivate a cheerful disposition we need to remember this is a command, our duty, our orders. We are to stop grumbling and complaining (Phil 2:14), but keep a song in our heart for all weather. To have a song of praise for rough times, for grief, for celebrating, for monotony… to "keep on singing even when the sun does not keep on shining." Do you have a song (or verses or a quote or poem) for good days and hard days? If not, start searching for one. If so, write it in your journal.

At the end of his rejoice command Paul gives us a how-to guide for rejoicing…

# Philippians 4
## joy in obedience

☐ In verses four through nine we have command after command from Paul. We're going to put these together like puzzle pieces. In the center of your page, write out verse seven (keep it fairly small), and draw a rectangle around it. You might draw a few pieces of a puzzle around the inner edge. This is to represent the finished puzzle, the promised result of practicing the commands Paul is going to give us.

☐ On your page, write out the command in verse four (small!) and draw a puzzle piece around the verse. Near the puzzle piece, write out what rejoicing in the Lord means in your life and what it looks like lived out.

☐ Write out verse five (small) and draw puzzle piece around it or near it. In this verse we have an important word. It is the word that immediately follows "Let your…" (In the NASB it is forbearing, in others it is gentleness, moderation, etc.) It is translated many different ways. The original Greek word was *epieikēs* and means gentleness, moderation, patient, considerate, reasonable, gracious. Look up the verse on Biblegateway.com and click through the different translations available and write out the English words this word is translated into. Draw puzzle pieces around them too.

☐ How can you let this be seen in your life? Go through each word you wrote down and choose one or two that stand out to you and write out what you could do to let each show in your life. What it might look like? This should SHOW in your life, in your face, in your thoughts, in your actions and attitudes. Don't get caught up in making a big long to-do list, remember this all is the work of the Spirit in your heart. Pray that He will scrape away enough of your own wants, fears, and desires so He can shine through.

☐ In verse six we have probably one of the most famous commands in Philippians. Write out just the first part (be anxious for nothing) and draw a puzzle piece around or near it. What things are you anxious about right now? List them near the verse.

☐ Write out the rest of verse six and draw a puzzle piece around or near it. Look back at the things you are anxious about and pray through them with supplication (seeking, asking, entreating) and thanksgiving… don't forget thanksgiving! Pray through each item and ask Him to help you leave it there with Him.

"[Satan] does not fear because we are eager and earnest Bible students-provided we are little in prayer. Satan laughs at our toiling, mocks at our wisdom, but trembles when we pray."
—Unknown, *The Kneeling Christian*

#JOURNALANDDOODLE

# Philippians 4
# growing in your thought life

☐ Turn to a new page in your journal and re-read chapter four.

☐ In verse eight, Paul gives us a list of the items we are to let our mind dwell on. Let's set up our page first, though. Draw a dividing line across the bottom of the page, leaving about a quarter of the page blank below the line. Now write each item (and its definition) in thought clouds all over your journal page. Near the thought clouds, write examples of things that have those characteristics—things that are lovely, honorable, pure, worthy of praise. Have fun brainstorming and listing!

We are surrounded by beautiful things. YOU are surrounded by them, just look at your list! But it takes real effort to focus on these things. Unfortunately our default mode is envy, want, or worry. We need to train ourselves to intentionally focus on these things.

☐ At the bottom quarter of your page, draw a jail cell window with bars. We need to train our mind to take every thought captive. Elisabeth Elliot said that the process of taking captives is never nice. Captives don't come willingly or easily. Taking captives is a violent job, just like taking thoughts captive. It's not going to happen naturally. How can you train your mind to take thoughts captive? Near your jail cell window write out some of the thoughts that you need to take captive and lock up such as fears, worries, negative self-talk, etc.

☐ Near each thought you need to take captive, list some ideas of how you can start doing it. This is putting the padlock on the shut cell door. Write out some truths, verses, or promises that you could think on instead.

☐ Turn to the next page in your journal and write out thought bubbles all over the page and list the same things again from verse eight in the bubbles. We are to let our minds dwell on and speak *truth*. Do you speak the truth to yourself?

☐ Next to each of these thought bubbles write out a few words or thoughts about what each would look like in your own life, or ideas on how to develop this in your life. For example, next to the "true" thought bubble, I'd write: "The Bible is truth. I need to know the truth." "I should not lie, exaggerate or deceive." Next to "honorable" I'd write "be above board in everything," "don't put myself in situations that could tempt myself or others," "be discerning in what I read and watch," etc. Work through all of the thought bubbles listing things that should be true of you.

☐ Choose one that you could focus on for the next month or so. Which one would make the biggest difference in your life right now? Draw a star next to it and write out some thoughts about how you will implement it and a prayer asking for help.

# Philippians 4
## growing in godliness

Paul ended this section by saying to watch him as he set the example. Like Paul, our goal should be to lead a life that can be a positive example to others. Paul wasn't bragging but was giving a real life example to follow.

☐ Write out the command in verse nine and doodle a pair of binoculars. We are to be watching and learning from other godly men and women. We must also be intentional to apply their examples to our lives. Then we can, like Paul, be speaking, hearing, and acting in a way that looks more and more like Christ.

☐ Can you think of people in your life right now who are an example of godly character? Make a list of who they are and what you see in them that you'd like to emulate.

☐ Are there people from the Bible or history who have been an inspiring example of godliness to you? Write out who they are and the example you would love to follow. (If you can, or if you have time, this would be a fun time to print and cut out pictures of these people and glue them in your journal.)

☐ Is there a way you can remove time-wasters in your life to make more time to read about other men and women in history who are excellent examples of godly living? I've made a list of great books to get you started. All are highly recommended reading! Write these down in your journal if you'd like (or on a to-read list) and add others you hear about or have been meaning to read.

**Short reads for busy women** (Think of these as introductions to these people.)
- Men of Faith Series by Bethany House Publishers
- Women of Faith Series by Bethany House Publishers
- Christian Heroes Series Janet and Geoff Benge (a bit longer books)

**WWII Heroes of the faith**
- Evidence Not Seen by Darlene Diebler
- The Hiding Place by Corrie Ten Boom
- Out of the Depths by Edgar Harrell
- If I Perish by Esther Ahn Kim

**Others**
- A Quiet Place in a Crazy World by Joni Eareckson Tada
- In the Land of Blue Burqas by Kate McCord
- Trial and Triumph : Stories from Church History by Richard Hannula

#JOURNALANDDOODLE

# Philippians 4
# joy in any situation

☐ Turn to a new page in your journal and re-read chapter four.

☐ In your journal, at the top of the page, write out verses 11-13.

☐ Draw two versions of Paul across from each other towards the top of your page. One should be in rags, and one dressed nicely. Under each version, write out the parts of verse 11-13 that apply. For example, under the Paul in rags I'd write: getting along in humble means, going hungry, suffering need, etc. Do this for both.

☐ In verse 12 Paul says he has learned the secret of this… what is that secret? (See verse 13.) Draw a key or a lock and write out what the secret is next to it.

☐ Look back to each version of Paul you doodled. What about your own life? How could you learn to be content as Paul was in both situations? Doodle a simple stick figure of yourself in both situations and write out specifics. Which situation do you find yourself more in right now? How can you be content there?

☐ Look back at your work on preparing for suffering in chapter three. Have you been thinking about that mindset? Review what you did there, and then on your current journal page re-write or add to your notes what you can do to prepare yourself to stand firm when trials hit.

*"Suffering is nothing more than the taking away of bad things or good things that the world offers for our enjoyment — reputation, esteem among peers, job, money, spouse, sexual life, children, friends, health, strength, sight, hearing, success, etc. When these things are taken away (by force or by circumstance or by choice), we suffer. But if we have followed Paul and the teaching of Jesus and have already counted them as loss for the surpassing value of gaining Christ, then we are prepared to suffer.*

*This means that if we treasure Jesus, then every aspect of suffering in our lives is losing something we have already declared as loss. If when you become a Christian you write a big red "LOSS" across all the things in the world except Christ, then when Christ calls you to forfeit some of those things, it is not strange or unexpected. The pain and the sorrow may be great. The tears may be many, as they were for Jesus in Gethsemane. But we will be prepared. We will know that the value of Christ surpasses all the things the world can offer and that in losing them we gain more of Christ."* -John Piper

#JOURNALANDDOODLE

# Philippians 4
## joy in giving

☐ Turn to a new page in your journal and re-read chapter four one more time.

☐ Around your page add some doodles that represent giving. A checkbook, cash, coins, gifts, a clock (to represent giving time), etc.

☐ Read slowly through verses 14-19 and write out everything you learn about giving in this section.

Some I got were: giving is sharing. Sharing in affliction and sharing in receiving. Giving is a blessing to those who give and to those who receive. Giving is a fragrant aroma, an acceptable sacrifice, and is well-pleasing to God. Giving changes both the giver and the recipient.

This reminds me of something our pastor once said around tax season. He said that every year when he is calculating his giving and deductions he really enjoys watching his tax bill get lower and lower… and often thinks "Man, I really wish I had given more!" Then he asked us if when we get to heaven, will we think the same thing? Will we see the difference our giving made and wish that we had given more? That is living and thinking in light of eternity. Giving whittles away our kingdom and helps build and grow God's kingdom here on earth.

I love this quote from Hunter Thompson *"Life should not be a journey to the grave with the intention of arriving safely in a pretty and well-preserved body, but rather to skid in broadside in a cloud of smoke, thoroughly used up, totally worn out, and loudly proclaiming "Wow! What a Ride!"* (Isn't that a great picture?!)

☐ Now it's your turn; how can you increase what you are giving now, in light of eternity (and the joy of the ride here on earth)? How can you open your heart more to sharing in affliction, sharing the gospel, giving a gift more than once, amply supplying others, and being a fragrant aroma, an acceptable sacrifice, well-pleasing to God? Brainstorm some ideas of how you can increase your giving (and remember, giving isn't solely relegated to money, but it definitely includes it). Some ideas:
- Set a specific monetary amount to give steadily each month, then try to meet and even exceed it.
- Double one meal a week (or month) and freeze it to give to sick or needy families in your church or neighborhood.
- Find a mission or charity you can really get behind and if you can't afford to give money, give prayer, or give time in serving with them.

Journal your ideas and how you can put them into action, then write a reminder note in your checkbook, budget, or on your calendar.

# Philippians 4
# joy in the glory of God

☐ Turn to a new page in your journal and re-read Philippians 4:20-23.

I cannot think of a better way to wrap up our time in Philippians than in pure worship and giving glory to the One who makes it possible!

☐ Let's take some time here to think about the word glory. Write the word glory big and bright in the middle of your journal page. You might want to make starbursts coming from it. The Greek word for glory is *doxa*. Does that remind you of anything? If you have a moment right now, do a search on YouTube for "doxology." Listen to a couple of your favorite versions and spend some time worshipping Him. (There are a lot of EXCELLENT versions on YouTube!)

☐ Now all over your journal page write out all the definitions of glory you can find. Here are the definitions listed from BlueLetterBible.org: A good opinion concerning one resulting in praise, honor and glory. Splendor, brightness (of the moon, sun, stars); magnificence; excellence; preeminence; dignity; grace; majesty; kingly majesty belonging to a supreme leader; majesty in the sense of the absolute perfection of the deity; a thing belonging to Christ; the kingly majesty of the Messiah; the absolutely perfect inward or personal Excellency of Christ; a most glorious condition; most exalted state.

In this one verse, we have so much to be joyful over and to give glory to Him about. He not only is all that you wrote out above, but He is also our Father. Our **Father!** Matthew Henry says, *"It is also a great privilege and encouragement to us to consider him as our Father, as one so nearly related and who bears so tender an affection towards us. We should look upon God, under all our weaknesses and fears, not as a tyrant or an enemy, but as a Father, who is disposed to pity us and help us."*

☐ Before we end, think about this; *"This Epistle was written by Paul when he was in prison, with iron fetters about his wrists; yet there is no iron in the Epistle. It is full of light, life, love, and joy, blended with traces of sorrow, yet with a holy delight that rises above his grief. "* -C. H. Spurgeon

☐ Wow. No matter our situation, no matter our condition, no matter our sins, our lack of joy… no matter what, we have SO MUCH to have joy in! May each of our lives be a life with no iron in it. May each one of us have a life full of light, love, and joy! At the bottom of your journal page, draw some broken chains and write out that quote from Spurgeon above.

#JOURNALANDDOODLE

# conclusion

## Wow! What an amazing time!

I'm so glad you came along on this ride with me. When I think back at all we've covered together, my mind is swirling!

If you're not quite ready to end your time in Philippians, here are a few suggestions for you to continue your journey.

☐ Flip back through your journal and review all you've covered. Add underlines, highlights, or "to-do" boxes in front of things that you know you need to do or work on.

☐ Make a new page with key ideas and main things that you've learned through your time in this book.

☐ In your Bible, title each page of Philippians with a key idea or summary for that page and highlight and underline verses that you chose for the study.

☐ Memorize the verses that stood out to you.

☐ Read through Philippians multiple times, keeping a tally in your Bible. You'd be shocked at how much of the book you automatically memorize by just reading it through repeatedly. If that seems crazy, read it through daily for a week, or ten times, or thirty, etc.

☐ Transcribe the entire book of Philippians in your journal. Each day write out however many verses you can in five minutes. Or write a specific number of verses a day. Make it slow and enjoy your time writing it out.

# bibliography

"Agape." PreceptAustin.org. Web. www.*PreceptAustin.org*

BlueLetterBible.org

"Epaphroditus." *International Standard Bible Encyclopaedia*, www.blueletterbible.org. Web. International Standard Bible Encyclopaedia

"Epaphroditus." PreceptAustin.org. Web. www.*PreceptAustin.org*

Lynch, John, McNicol, Bruce, *The Cure: What if God isn't who you think He is and neither are you?*, Trueface, April 2016

Maclaren, Alexander. "Expositions of Holy Scripture" *Bible Hub*. Web.

Philippians Illustrations. PreceptAustin.org. Web. www.*PreceptAustin.org*

Pink, A.W. PreceptAustin.org. Web. www.*PreceptAustin.org*

"Timothy." Easton's Bible Dictionary. New York: Thomas Nelson, 1894.

# Find all the Journal and Doodle Bible Studies

# www.stonesoupforfive.com

(There's also a whole library of free doodles at www.stonesoupforfive.com)

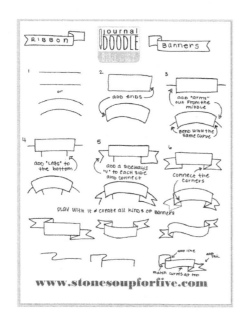